D1279316

FOR THE *Rights* OF MEN

FOR THE
Rights
OF MEN

by
CARL CARMER

Essay Index Reprint Series

BOOKS FOR LIBRARIES PRESS
FREEPORT, NEW YORK

STANDARD BOOK NUMBER:

8369-1175-X

LIBRARY OF CONGRESS CATALOG CARD NUMBER:

75-86740

PRINTED IN THE UNITED STATES OF AMERICA

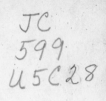

CONTENTS

Banished from Massachusetts, 1660. — Drawing by E. A. Abbey.

John Peter Zenger

We Americans are proud that the Pilgrim Fathers and the Puritans who soon followed them dared the Atlantic for the chance to worship God in their own way. Every Fourth of July, every Decoration Day, every Pioneer Picnic Day, and on the birthdays of Washington and Lincoln, our speechmakers repeat the story with a good deal of eloquent embroidery. Usually they try to give us the idea that we have had freedom of worship and the other freedoms that go with it—freedom of speech, freedom of the press, freedom of assembly—ever since. We are willing to cheer but we are not fooled. When we get down to brass tacks we know that the Pilgrims were human and likely at times to get excited and forget the very things they stood for—just like many of us.

Hardly a score of years had passed before these early American fugitives from religious persecutions were themselves persecuting peaceful people. Some of our ancestors even condemned books for expressing bad ideas, convicted them, and had them lashed by the public hangman before they were burned. Other Puritans tried, convicted, and sentenced the Reverend John Dunster, first president of Harvard College, because he disagreed with the majority about the baptism of babies. Bostonians hanged Mary Dyer on the Common because she would not leave the colony although she had been banished for being a Quaker.

One thing we have learned from such tragedies as these is that the fight for the rights of the individual common man is never won. The price we pay for those rights is that we must always be on our guard against their enemies. Sometimes we find the foe within us—in our own weak failure to give people who disagree with us the rights we demand for ourselves. Sometimes we find him in the smooth arguer against the American way of life who says we would all be better off if we traded our freedom for the alleged benefits of a dictatorship. One fact gives us courage. America, champion of the rights of man, has never lost the battle. She has had her moments of temporary defeat, 'but, like her great naval hero, John Paul Jones, in such moments she has "just begun to fight."

When English settlers first came here they brought with them the idea of the "rights of a free-born Englishman." Within them was the spirit of the men who in the year 1215 wrote the first great statement of those rights, the Magna Carta. But this spirit which gave people their human rights through a contract with those who governed them, was not enough. Probably these new Americans got another feeling about their rights from their religion. It taught that every man had at the beginning of his life a soul that was the equal of the soul of every other man. On this—a kind of pure white blank—he could write his own ticket for heaven or hell. It was easy to argue from this that people come into the world equal in other ways, too: that a man is born with natural rights. To this day the hard-boiled thinkers, people who sneer at ideals, keep shouting that nobody has any rights except those his neighbors let him have. But Americans go about their business smiling. No matter how much noise the shouters make, Americans say that a man is born with rights that should not be taken from him. They say that these are a part of the dignity and worth of being born a man. They say that it may not sound logical but they are satisfied to believe that Thomas Jefferson was right when he put to paper the words "All men are created equal." This was the contribution of the first Americans to the history of man's fight for the freedom of the individual. We are still proud of it.

Ever since we got these two ideas in our heads—that men can reserve certain rights to themselves in the agreements made with those who govern them and that men are born with natural rights—Americans have been acting on the theory that a man can do what he pleases as long as he does not break laws he and his neighbors have made for their own protection. Let anybody try to stop him and he answers with the nation's favorite come-back: "It's a free country, isn't it?"

Sometimes an answer like that has caused trouble. In Massachusetts in 1635 Roger Williams spoke up for a man's right to be an infidel if he felt that way. His neighbors tried him and sentenced him to be deported to England. He got away to the Indians and when the lilacs were blooming at the head of Narragansett Bay he built some houses for himself and those who believed as he did. He called the little settlement Providence. Thus the state of Rhode Island began in democracy and religious freedom. Today we remember the name of Roger Williams and we forget the names of those who hated him and banished him because his thoughts were not their thoughts. We remember, too, the name of Anne Hutchinson—"Scarlet Anne"— who was sent away from the Massachusetts Colony for giving voice to religious beliefs not held by the majority. Signs along the New York State road on which she built her house—now the Hutchinson River Parkway—remind thousands of Westchester County citizens every day of the story of her exile and of her death at the hands of hostile Indians.

This girl is being accused of witchcraft, for which women were burned in early America.

Culver Service

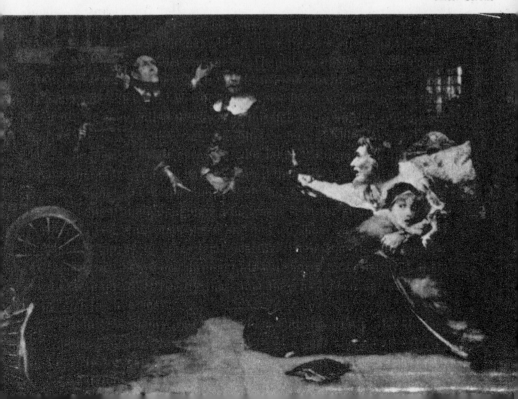

Roger Williams in the forest.

Freedom of worship was not the only right that our liberty-seeking forebears denied to those who disagreed with them. On an early fall day in 1690 Benjamin Harris, who ran a coffee house in Boston, published and handed out the first American newspaper, *Publick Occurrences, Both Forreign and Domestick*. It said among other things that the Mohawk Indians should not be used as soldiers in the war against French Canada because they were savage and cruel, "too barbarous for any English to approve." It took the Governor and Council of the Colony just three days to get out an order calling in all copies of the paper and forbidding the printing of further issues.

Little more than thirty years later this same Boston Council ordered James Franklin of Hartford, Connecticut, put in jail for printing in his paper, the *New England Courant*, ideas which they said were in "contempt of the authorities." While James was in jail his little sixteen-year-old half brother ran the paper by himself. Bravely young Benjamin Franklin printed what he had to say against his brother's imprisonment. "Without freedom of thought," he wrote, "there can be no such thing as wisdom, and no such thing as public liberty without freedom of speech."

The most famous of all such stories—and the best—is the tale of the poor German refugee John Peter Zenger.

In the days before the American Revolution, empires sometimes forgot that citizens of their colonies deserved the same rights as citizens of the mother countries. Even the New Amsterdam Dutch, who were in many respects fairly reasonable, made life pretty hard for Roman Catholics and Quakers. The English, who took up governing New York where the Dutch left off, sent over a series of governors who robbed the people of more and more of their rights. In 1734 Peter Zenger began to kick about this in his newspaper, the *New York Weekly Journal*. Governor William Cosby had him arrested and thrown into jail. There for nine months he stayed. With his wife's help he kept the paper going—dictating his editorials through a hole in the door of his cell. Then the Governor, in true dictator fashion, disbarred Zenger's lawyers, and ruled that they could not defend him. Things looked pretty black for freedom of the press in New York about then.

John Peter Zenger was tried in the old town hall. It stood on Wall Street where the subtreasury building is now. The lawyer for the Governor called John Peter some pretty nasty names and everybody there could see that the judge was on the Governor's side. All seemed fixed for a conviction when suddenly an old man got up to speak for the defense. The courtroom audience gasped. It was white-haired, eighty-year-old Andrew Hamilton—the finest lawyer in all the colonies. Though his body was weak with age, he had come all the way

Whipping of Quakers at the cart's tail in Boston.

from Philadelphia to speak for the rights of Peter Zenger and the rights of all men. For a good many years now when Americans have wanted to say something special about a man's brains they have said, "He's as smart as a Philadelphia lawyer." Maybe that comes all the way from old Andrew Hamilton's speech on that day. Whether it does or not, we know that it was a great speech.

"Men who injure and oppress the people under their administration," said Andrew Hamilton sternly, "provoke them to cry out and complain, and then make that very complaint the foundation for new oppressions. . . . The question before the court and you, gentlemen of the jury, is not of small and private concern; it is not the cause of a poor printer, nor of New York alone, which you are trying. No! . . . It is the best cause: it is the cause of liberty!"

When old Mr. Hamilton had finished his speech, there was sudden silence. The jury rose, then, and slowly made their way from the hot courtroom. Their faces were grave and troubled.

The crowd fidgeted in their seats. The half-light of the end of day blurred the empty bench where the jurors had sat. A door opened and suddenly the bench was full again. Eagerly the spectators peered into the faces of the jurors, seeking some indication of what the verdict would be. But the features of Jack Bell, Ben Hildreth, Tom Hunt, Sam Weaver, and their fellow-jurors gave no sign. Then the foreman spoke:

"We find the defendant, John Peter Zenger, not guilty."

The roar of the crowd seemed to shake the courtroom. Vainly the angry judge rapped for order, demanding silence. The waiting people outside in Wall Street realized that they had gained a victory and shouted their joy. Broadway answered with resounding cheers. In the never-ceasing war for human rights Andrew Hamilton's great argument had won a battle. The aged lawyer knew that there would be other such battles long after his death. But one man's rights had been secured. Peter Zenger could now print and distribute his opinions without being thrown into jail. The outcome of the fight had been a good beginning. Andrew Hamilton was content. He had spoken for the people and the people had won.

But, in spite of Zenger's victory, the British continued to disregard the civil rights of the Americans. For thirty years the colonists complained. Then they got around to doing something about it. In 1764 James Otis wrote a declaration called "The Rights of the British Colonists." That was the beginning. The Americans had something to go by. Ten years later they were ready to say to England: "Give us our rights or we'll take them." In those ten years Massachusetts had listed her grievances in a series of Resolves that foreshadowed the Declaration of Independence; Virginia had readied herself to announce her own Bill of Rights; Americans everywhere had hailed John Wilkes, the London publisher who had dared to print attacks on governmental abuses and had gone to jail for his convictions. Americans were now prepared to risk their lives and fortunes for the rights of men.

Culver Service

AndrewHamilton.

"Wilkes and Liberty!" was the toast in Hartford and Philadelphia,
Baltimore and Charleston. Every colony was in a white heat of anger
over the British government's denial of the rights of the individual.

We know what happened. There is no need to tell the story of the
Revolution. It need only be pointed out that, as in all wars, the individual lost his civil rights. The fighters for American freedom persecuted the Tories cruelly—just as all war parties persecute those who
disagree with them. After the war was over, men who had honestly
believed the colonies should stay under the British Crown were tarred
and feathered, ridden on rails, even hanged. The first efforts of the
believers in human rights in the new country were toward re-estab-
lishing the liberty for which the fight had been made. It had all but
disappeared. The Revolution had created a new nation. It had not
established a free democracy. The building of a country based on
that ideal was the job ahead.

As we read today of the sad failures of certain people in the past
to respect the rights of others, we are likely to think of ourselves as
folks pretty much like those who got into trouble for sticking to their
guns. We become angry with the majorities that made the trouble.
We need to ask ourselves occasionally where we stand today—which

The trial of Peter Zenger.

Culver Service

Hamilton and the people.

side would we really have been on? Do we praise the courage of
unpopular Roger Williams and of despised Anne Hutchinson and
at the same time deny the rights of believers in unpopular causes to
be heard? If we do, we know that it is we who act in an un-American
way, not those who speak as their consciences tell them. No matter
how wrong we may consider our fellow citizens, we know that belief
in the American tradition requires that we let them speak.

Bill Prendergast and Mehitabel Wing were married in the Quaker meetinghouse.

2

Land of His Own

"My own piece of land." These words tell every farmer's dream
—the dream that once brought men from many nations to the shores
of a new country—America. But the folks who want to eat their cake
and have it too are always on the job and not easily outdone. That's
what the redheaded Kilkenny Irishman Bill Prendergast found out
around 1760 when he began to search the country near the Hudson
River for a few acres that lay nice to the morning sun.

He found them all right—looking as green now as they did the
first day Bill set eyes on them. People who live near Pawling,
New York, play golf on them today. But Bill worked hard on them
—turning the green under to seed the brown earth in spring, reaping
the yellow grain at summer's end.

Bill wanted to own that land—as any farmer wants to own the
field he plows—but he found out he couldn't, not even if he saved
enough money to buy it. Frederick Phillipse, a fat rich fellow who
called himself Lord of Phillipse Manor and who lived in a fancy
house at Yonkers, had got the British king to hand those acres and
hundreds of thousands more over to him and he would not sell. He
told Bill he would let him have a long lease on a few acres if Bill
would pay him four pounds a year for the privilege, work for him
several days out of every year, and bring him ten hens and a dozen
bushels of wheat every rent day. Bill did not like the idea but he
had fallen in love with a pretty sixteen-year-old miss who lived high
up above his farm in a big house at the top of Quaker Hill and so he
finally agreed.

It did not take Bill Prendergast long after he had started farming
to persuade Mehitabel Wing to marry him. He just kept making
tracks up the hill to see her and he was so smart and obliging around

the Wing place that even her Quaker parents did not object—and that was a pretty good record for a Kilkenny Irishman. They were married in the Quaker meetinghouse. You can still see it if you go to the top of Quaker Hill. It has been changed a little but the inside is about the same as it was then.

The story about Bill and Mehitabel and their fight to own their farm really begins about twelve years after the wedding. Crops had not been too good in all that time and the number of mouths for them to feed had grown a bit—with two sons already on hand and a third likely to be before long.

Bill had spent a long hard day waiting in line with hundreds of other tenant farmers to pay off the Lord of Phillipse Manor with his hens and wheat. Every time Bill got a little ahead, along came rent day and fat Frederick took away what Bill had saved. When he finally reached the manor lord's desk he had to wait while Frederick waddled off to take care of something or other. And there on the desk in front of him lay a paper that told Bill something. It was a statement of Frederick Phillipse's account with the British king and it said that for all his hundreds of thousands of acres fat Frederick paid a rent

Bill Prendergast told
his farmer-neighbors.

of four pounds—just what Bill had been paying for his little farm.

I do not need to tell you that Bill's temper took hold of him. You know how a Kilkenny Irishman is—or any descendant of a Kilkenny Irishman for that matter. Bill went home and when he found out that young Jedediah Prendergast had just been born, the mixture of his pride in his new son and his anger at fat Frederick got his temper up to the boiling point. He went out into the Hudson Valley and told all his farmer-neighbors just what sort of scoundrel fat Frederick was. The farmers became almost as angry as Bill and they said, "You just lead us, Farmer Prendergast, and we'll attend to this fellow and all the rest of these manor lords that oppress poor and honest farmers with high rents." All of a sudden Bill Prendergast found himself at the head of an army of nearly a thousand wild Westchester farmers who had had enough of this feudal monkey business about manor lords who would not sell a decent man enough soil to be buried in.

Then, with Bill Prendergast waving a sword as he led them on, the whole crowd started marching down the river road to New York to tell the Governor of the province all about it. On the way they emptied all the jails, releasing poor farmers who had been imprisoned because they couldn't pay their rent. Whenever they found a flint-hearted landlord or a judge who was hard on farmers they freshened him up a bit by tossing him into the nearest mill pond. Every day or so, riders from the manor lords galloped into the city to tell the Governor what was happening. The people of New York were frightened. There were only ten thousand folks in the whole city and a thousand Westchester farmers seemed like quite a lot of farmers.

When Bill Prendergast's army reached the Harlem River they stopped there and sent six polite farmers into town to tell Governor Harry Moore how things were with them. The Governor had sense enough to talk politely to them and say that if they had any grievances something ought to be done. Then, before the farmers said good-by, he showed them a couple of regiments of red-coated grenadiers drawn up at the Battery.

When the six had recrossed the Harlem and told their story, Bill Prendergast and the rest of the leaders decided that maybe the best thing to do was to go back home and avoid trouble. They did just that—stopping here and there to empty a jail of rent-debtors.

But the manor lords had begun to make things hot for Governor Moore. They said that if he knew what was good for him he would have those insolent farmers arrested and punished. And before the farmers knew much about it, a regiment of grenadiers had landed at Poughkeepsie and they were now hurrying after Bill Prendergast. Not being professional soldiers most of the farmers went home, but about fifty stayed with Bill and fortified themselves in the old meetinghouse where he had married Mehitabel. They remained there all one night and then, in the morning, seeing that the place was surrounded by redcoats, they gave up and marched out under a flag of truce—that is, all except Bill Prendergast. They had sent him out of harm's way during the night.

This becomes Mehitabel's story for a while now. William had got himself into a peck of trouble and it was time for his wife to do something about it. The first thing she did was to take the baby and his two brothers to their grandmother's house on top of Quaker Hill. Then she went out and found William. She persuaded him that he could not play a lone hand and had better give himself up. When that slip of a woman brought in the terrible outlaw whom the regiment of redcoats could not catch, the major was embarrassed.

The grenadiers did not dare put William in the Poughkeepsie jail that he had already emptied a couple of times. They rushed him to prison in New York. Then, at the July sessions of the court, the Attorney General of the province saw to it that he was indicted for high treason.

Mehitabel knew that this meant death for her husband if he were convicted. When they brought William back upriver she was waiting at the dock.

Then began one of the strangest trials in history. As that grim business started, Mehitabel Prendergast assumed that she was in the courtroom to help her husband and no one said her nay. She told the Chief Justice of the court and his associates and the jury of freeholders that her husband was more sinned against than sinning. She said he had been "esteemed a sober, honest and industrious farmer, much beloved by his neighbors." The Poughkeepsie reporter of the *New York Gazette or Weekly Post Boy* sent inspired accounts downriver, and excited New Yorkers found themselves reading about a new heroine: ". . . solicitously attentive to every particular and without the least Impertinence or Indecorum of Behaviour, sedately anxious for her husband, she never failed to make every remark that might tend to extenuate the Offence and put his conduct in the most favorable point of view not suffering one Circumstance that could be collected from the evidence or thought in his Favour to escape the Notice of the Court and the Jury.

"And when he came to make his Defence she stood behind him, reminded him of and suggested to him everything that could be mentioned to his advantage."

At last the temper of the Attorney General grew short and he began to growl.

Mehitabel defended her husband.

"Your Lordship, I move you that this woman be removed from the court, lest she too much influence the jury."

"She does not disturb the court," said the Chief Justice trying to look solemn, "nor does she speak unreasonably."

"Your Lordship, I do not think that she should speak at all, and I fear her very looks may too much influence the jury."

"You might as well move that the Prisoner himself be covered with a veil for the same reason," snapped the Chief Justice.

But Mehitabel, though she fought the good fight, knew that she had not a chance. A jury of landowners, with a board of judges who were friends of the manor lords, would bring in only one decision. She was ready for her next action as the foreman was saying the awful word "Guilty," even as the Chief Justice was uttering the fearful sentence:

". . . that the Prisoner . . . shall be hanged by the neck, and then shall be cut down alive . . . and his Entrails shall be cut from his body and shall be burned in his sight and his head shall be cut off and his body shall be divided into four parts."

"May God have mercy on my soul," said William Prendergast in despair.

Mehitabel kissed her husband and rushed from the courtroom. The trial had lasted twenty-four hours but she had no thought of fatigue. There was still one desperate chance to save her husband's life and she was taking it. Eighty miles away in the palace at the Battery in New York lived Governor Harry Moore. She would beg him for a reprieve, persuade him to recommend to King George that her husband be pardoned.

Down the King's Road she galloped—racing her image in the clear water of the river—past Fishkill and Oscawanna Creek, past Peekskill, past the green slopes of the Manitou Mountains, past Tappan Bay, past King's Ferry and Tarrytown, past the great Phillipse Manor House where fat Frederick lived richly on the rents of poor men like her husband, and sometimes caused their deaths, and finally there was the ribbon of the Harlem below her and the slow little ferry. Down the full length of Manhattan she dashed—begging even as she dismounted that she might see the Governor.

Sir Harry could never resist a pretty woman.

Mehitabel's descendants say (and they should know) that she was no sooner in Sir Harry Moore's presence then she strode up and down in her pretty blue-striped linen gown (borrowed from her sister for the occasion) and her tears and her entreaties were so heart-rending that Sir Harry—who could never resist a pretty woman in distress—himself burst into tears and swore her husband should not suffer. She got him to put that in writing and then she started back. She knew that she would be lucky to arrive before the enraged farmers of the Hudson Valley had once more emptied the Poughkeepsie jail and rescued William Prendergast. And she knew that if they did, the reprieve would be of no value and the next time the grenadiers caught William they would hang him. So once more she urged her husband's gallant horse over the long eighty-mile stretch. She got back in time—the farmers were just leading Bill out of the jail when she dashed up. She had saved her husband's life, she had persuaded the Governor to ask the King for his pardon, she had ridden a hundred and sixty miles on horseback—and all in less than three days!

If this were not a true story it would end here. But you and I know that life goes beyond story endings—and you and I like to know what happened afterwards. The answer is—plenty. William got his pardon all right and came home. And Mehitabel bore him ten more children—four more sons and six daughters for a grand total of thirteen. But, as the years went by and the family grew up, William and Mehitabel never gave up the idea that one day they would have a "piece of land of their own." They just did not feel right on another man's land. William was seventy-eight and Mehitabel was sixty-seven before they were ready to start out to look for that piece of land. By that time there were many grandchildren and it took four covered Conestoga wagons with four horses hitched to each wagon to get all the twenty-nine Prendergasts and their in-laws under way. Mehitabel sat in a barouche in the rear and kept her eye on things.

They built their home — with the help of the family.

They started south first. When they reached Wheeling, Pennsylvania, they bought a flatboat, drove their wagons on it, and floated all the way to Louisville, Kentucky. Then they started cross-country again and went as far as Duck Creek, near Nashville, Tennessee, before they decided they would rather live back in their home state · after all. So they rolled northwards through Ohio and on until, back in New York State, they saw the blue waters of Chautauqua Lake. There, at the northwest corner of the lake, William and Mehitabel found what they had been looking for all their lives—"a piece of land of their own." On it they built their house—with the help of the family. One of their daughters who was a spinster and one who was a widow lived with them there and helped them farm. The rest of the family moved to other land near-by. Their son James, founder of Jamestown, New York, brought his wife for a long visit with them in the autumn of 1810. By that time they had been farming their own land for five years.

William was eighty-four that winter and the snows of. February proved too much for him. Mehitabel lived a year and a half after he left her. In the early autumn of 1812, just forty-six years from the day of her long ride, she went once more to her husband. They lie side by side in the cemetery near Chautauqua Lake—two people who risked their lives, who gladly went through sorrow and pain and hardship to gain a right that you and I take for granted in this free country—the right to have "a piece of land of your own."

George Clinton

3

After the Revolution

From the country's very beginnings to now, Americans have had proud faith in their own common sense. They have believed that a number of good minds at work on a question will find a better answer to it than any single mind could find. They have believed from the first in training minds to be aware of the past, alert in the present. Once a young American has had a reasonable amount of such training our idea has been to turn him loose. We are satisfied that he can recognize foolishness when he hears it or reads it. We are satisfied, too, that with his trained and free mind he is more likely to come out with a good productive idea than some poor devil who has been brought up to believe there is only one way to skin a cat—the boss's way.

We have learned, too, that it is a good thing to let all the folks we call fools speak their pieces. For one thing, it sometimes turns out that they are on our side and thinking a little ahead of us. We know what the majority thought of Jesus Christ. And if we do not know what the ruling American party, the Federalists, thought about Thomas Jefferson and his ideas on building a democracy of free and equal men here, we ought to find out. They did not pull their punches.

Experience has taught us that another good reason for letting a foolish man talk rather than suppressing him is that, even if his ideas are wild and possibly dangerous, we know where he is and what he thinks. Like the rattlesnake, he sounds off and gives a chance for back talk. A dangerous idea blatted by an idiot from a soapbox signifies nothing. Often enough the idiot is satisfied to take it all out in talk. But warn him that he will be arrested if he approaches a soapbox, and his addled brain will seek revenge in secret meetings with others of his kind and in plotting for rebellious action. Conspiracy feeds on suppression. If we must have enemies within our gates, it is better to know who they are, how they think, what they plan, rather than blindly to wait for the stab in the back.

When they were debating adoption of our Constitution way back in 1788, the elected representatives of our state governments brought up arguments like these and came to the same conclusions. The Constitution does not protect the very liberties for which we have been fighting, they cried. We will not vote for it unless it does.

At the convention in Poughkeepsie, General George Clinton—big old George, whose Hudson Valley troops had followed him devotedly throughout the Revolution because he was a farmer like themselves —led the battle against adopting a constitution which contained no bill of rights. He was fighting on familiar ground. He had been brought up on the Hudson's west bank, the free and democratic bank where a man could own his own farm and not have to pay feudal manor rents to the east-bank aristocrats, landlords of the great estates. Just a few miles downriver he had risked his life and lost the seat of his pants when he escaped from the British by sliding on his rump from the top of a steep mountain to the bottom.

The Federalists, led by Alexander Hamilton, claimed they won the fight against George, for the Constitution was adopted as it stood. But the farmers "knew different." In return for setting their seal of approval on the Constitution, they had received the promise that its first amendments would give them the rights they had won.

When the day came for those promises to be kept, however, the members of the Federalist Party were not eager to keep their bargain. On June 8, 1789, the House of Representatives met in the national capitol in New York and James Madison brought up the question of amendments to guard the rights of individuals in the new nation. The legislatures of the states had made no less than a hundred and thirty suggestions for guarantees to be included in the American Bill of Rights. That was typical of the American way of doing business. They were not going to miss having any rights they thought they should have. Madison had boiled the lot of them down in the kettle of his own common sense to just nine, and the fourth of these was

Celebrating the ratification of the Constitution by New York State.

the most important because it held nearly all the ideas contained in that part of our Constitution we know now as the Bill of Rights.

As soon as Madison had presented the nine suggestions, the Federalist members jumped to their feet and yelled for a chance to speak. The Constitution had been adopted as complete, they shouted, and it would be unwise to weaken it by adding amendments. It was improper, it was radical, it was revolutionary to give the people such powers. But the objectors were about to see the people of the United States put their democracy into action. Through their representatives they were saying that the human rights for which they had fought and won a war must be given them here and now.

The opposition put up a great fight. They shouted, they stomped, they pooh-poohed, they delayed. It took a whole month and more for the champions of individual liberty to have a committee appointed to consider amendments, but it took the committee, made up of one man from each state, just one week to bring in a report. The enemies of civil liberty had the report laid on the table for more than two weeks, but they could not hold out any longer. On August 13 the report was taken up and from then on for nine hot days, while tempers stretched to the breaking point and men let their minds become twisted by anger and prejudice, the debate went on. On the 22nd of August the American Bill of Rights was passed in the House of Representatives and sent on to the Senate. The Senate quickly passed it and referred it to the states for confirmation. Before Christmas the articles of the Bill of Rights were a part of the Constitution.

No laws had ever been more completely the result of the opinions of a people as a whole. There were echoes of Virginia in them—echoes of Patrick Henry shouting "Give me liberty or give me death," of George Mason scratching away with his quill in 1776 to pen the Virginia Bill of Rights. There were echoes from sunny South Carolina, from bleak and rocky Maine, from stern and liberty-loving Massachusetts. These words were written in the shadow of a forest of liberty poles while the songs of the people's victory still rang in the ears of the writer. From all the states came the cry that the sacrifices of Bunker Hill and Valley Forge should not have been made in vain. Independence from England was not enough if it merely meant a substitution of a new tyranny for the old.

The people had the bit in their teeth and were running away. They had an idea—an idea so radical and revolutionary that Russia refused to grant this mad new country recognition as a nation among nations. It was an idea so new that in their enthusiasm for it they found it hard to explain its meaning. Seven decades and more would pass before an American would sum it up in sure and deathless words—"government of the people, by the people, for the people."

But in those more than seventy years before Abraham Lincoln was to speak at Gettysburg many a battle for human rights was to be fought—for the enemy never sleeps. Hardly had the rejoicing over the passage of the Bill of Rights ended than the liberties it guaranteed were in danger. Though the first of the ten articles of the bill reads, "Congress shall make no law respecting an establishment of religion, or prohibiting the free exercise thereof," the individual states were already denying their citizens full religious freedom.

New Hampshire, Connecticut, New Jersey, Georgia, North Carolina, and South Carolina permitted only Protestants to become citizens. In Maryland only Christians could vote. Pennsylvania required those who would exercise their constitutional rights to swear that they believed in the divine inspiration of the Bible. Delaware demanded that they declare their belief in the Trinity.

At the same time the Federalist Party, then in power, tried to establish an aristocratic tradition in America. John Adams came out flat-footed for a monarchy. "Take away thrones and crowns from among men," he wrote, "and there will soon be an end of all dominion and justice." Alexander Hamilton spoke out for government by the rich and wellborn: "The people are turbulent and changing, they seldom judge or determine right." The dignitaries of Washington's second administration, his "court circle," began to call themselves Lords and Ladies. At no time in our history were the personal rights of a common man in greater peril than in the decade immediately after those rights had been made a part of the Federal Constitution.

But always in our history, when the foes of human rights have

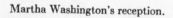

Martha Washington's reception.

Culver Service

become most powerful, brave champions have led the people in slashing counterattacks to victory. In a hostile cabinet Jefferson fought for the idea he was later to express in his first inaugural address: "A wise and frugal government which shall restrain men from injuring one another, which shall leave them otherwise free to regulate their own pursuits of industry and improvement, and shall not take from the mouth of labor the bread it has earned." Loyally, Philip Freneau, hero poet of the Revolution, supported this stand, lashing out at the Federalists with biting rhymes.

"In ten short years, of freedom weary grown
The State, Republic, sickens for a throne."

Thomas Paine.

Culver Service

Tom Paine, who had already proved his pen mightier than many a British sword, plunged, body, boots, and breeches, into this new revolution against American autocrats who would deny civil rights to their fellowmen. Eagerly he contradicted Hamilton: "As far as my experience in public life extends, I have ever observed that the great mass of people are always just, both in their intentions and their object." The people of America closed in behind these leaders demanding that the dream for which they had fought the War for Independence be allowed to come true.

The answers of the Federalists grew shriller and shriller. Finally, they took to the last and weakest trick of the man who has run out of arguments—name-calling. These Democrat-Republicans, they shouted, were dangerous radicals, immoral lowborn scum, rabble-rousers, anarchists, atheists. The Federalists should have known better. The "rich and wellborn" are hardly ever as clever at calling names as the farmer and the shoemaker. The Federalists got much better than they sent. Enraged, they overstepped themselves as pretenders to dictatorial powers have always done. Charging that the democratic masses were identifying themselves with the radical, bloodthirsty mobs that had made a horror out of the French Revolution and that the national government was endangered thereby, the Federalists jammed through Congress those notorious boomerangs known as the Alien and Sedition Acts.

Alexander Hamilton.

4

Victories in Hudson

Unhappily, time and again in the years of our existence as a nation Americans have been called upon to defend the civil rights of men who were far from admirable as personalities, men whose opinions were to their way of thinking far from sound, men whom most honest citizens might regard with dislike if not mistrust.

Yet so firmly do Americans believe in the Bill of Rights, these unpopular fellows have found champions among the best of our citizens. More than once the lawyer fighting in court for the civil rights of his client has been aware that he disagreed with the man's every opinion and that as a person he had only contempt for him. Yet, because this client was an American citizen deprived of liberties granted him by the Constitution the lawyer has continued the fight bravely.

It may reasonably be wondered, then, what was the state of mind of Alexander Hamilton when he set out in 1804 for the little city of Hudson, there to defend Printer Harry Croswell before the Supreme Court of the State of New York. Croswell had been charged with having scandalized, slandered and abused President Thomas Jefferson and with having alienated from him the obedience, fidelity and allegiance of the citizens of the state. Hamilton knew well that what Croswell had printed about Jefferson was violent and abusive and colored by extreme prejudice. But a principle was involved, the same principle that had led Hamilton to fight the Sedition Bill which his own party, the Federalists, had passed with disastrous results to themselves a few years before.

Now the American political scene whirled suddenly upside down. The bitter words of a Federalist editor in a small, upstate city had burned the Democrat-Republicans like hot cinders under their collars.

Thomas Jefferson.

Losing control of their tempers these members of the party that had championed the rights of the common man had sought and obtained an indictment against Harry Croswell just as their opponents had done in the case of Matthew Lyon who was jailed for a similar offense when John Adams was President.

Spectators at that trial, sitting in the chilly courtroom through the snowy days of early February expected that Croswell, like Lyon, would be convicted and imprisoned. They were sure of this outcome when General Ambrose Spencer had finished his fiery attack on the hotheaded young editor. The speech of William W. Van Ness, associated with Hamilton in Croswell's defense, did not help matters much. Chief Justice Morgan Lewis and the other judges stirred uneasily. The audience felt that the cause of freedom of the press in the United States was about to be defeated. Then Alexander Hamilton, 47 years old and at the height of his powers, rose to make his last courtroom speech. (Five months later he lay dying on the little greensward duelling field at Weehawken.)

The people who heard him that day remembered it years afterward and said that as he spoke it seemed as if he knew that he had little time left and that he wanted to get in his best licks for freedom of the American press. Harry Croswell meant little to him personally but the right of a newspaper to print its editor's beliefs meant a great deal.

The reporter for the *New York Post* sent downriver his account of that speech. "Then came the great, the powerful Hamilton. . . . No language can convey an adequate idea of the astonishing power evinced by him. The audience was numerous . . . and the effect on them was electric. . . . As a profound commentary on the science and practice of government, it has never been surpassed."

He said that a printer had the right to publish things he believed in even if they were against the government just as long as his ideas were sincere and his purposes were justifiable. He said that if a man were charged with abusing this liberty he had a right to a court trial by jury and that the members of that jury should be given the power not only to decide what were the facts of the case but also to judge what his motives were and whether he acted in good faith.

Alexander Hamilton rose to make his last courtroom speech.

His speech so influenced the justices who heard the case that two of the four voted for acquittal. Croswell came out of his ordeal scot free, for Alexander Hamilton had not merely ended his prosecution for him by winning the tie vote. Hamilton had so roused public opinion that within a short time a bill which sharply defined libel and made clear the rights of the press to criticize government officers was passed by the Federal Congress. Because a great American had put aside whatever personal feeling and prejudice he might have had against a silly defendant, the people of the United States had declared their belief in the freedom asserted in the Bill of Rights.

The true American of today does not forget these things. He does not identify the lawyer with the client. He knows that the champion of civil liberty may personally dislike the man he defends, may feel that he is completely mistaken in his opinions. Every true American defends the right of every citizen to say or print or act upon his beliefs. The American Presbyterian and the Roman Catholic defend the little sects like Jehovah's Witnesses who even now are being persecuted by misled and un-American "patriots" in some states because their thinking (considered mistaken if not slightly cracked by most people of the country) brings them to the conclusion that in saluting the symbols of their country's government they deny the supreme authority of their God. The United States has not for many generations demanded military service from citizens whose consciences will not let them give it. The pacifist Quakers of America have long been among our most valued and respected citizens. We who believe in American ideals will not deny the civil rights of Jehovah's Witnesses simply because we like them less than we like Quakers.

But the little city of Hudson, lying in the shadow of the Taghanick Mountains and looking across the great Hudson River to the purple Catskills, had not seen the end of the nation's battle to keep its promise of civil freedom for American citizens.

Thirty-two years after Alexander Hamilton's impassioned defense of Harry Croswell the people of the town saw eight of their neighbors, shoemakers all, file into the old courthouse and sit in the seats of prisoners. They had been indicted on a charge of conspiracy for forming, on September 15, 1835, "The United Society of Journeymen Cordwainers of the City of Hudson" and agreeing that no member of the society should work for less wages than those it should decide upon nor for any boss who should employ anyone not a member of the society.

Other societies like this had been formed long before these shoemakers had banded together. Members had been indicted and tried on like charges. All defendants had been found guilty. With the precedent of a Supreme Court decision on their side (a decision based in turn on English law), Prosecuting Attorneys Sutherland and Hogeboom looked for an easy victory. Josiah Sutherland spoke first. These shoemakers had no right to meet together to fix prices by combina-

The eight shoemakers filed into the old courthouse.

tion, he shouted. "The tendency of these societies," he went on sternly, "is to restrain the free circulation of wealth through the country; and the powerful arm of the law has the right to put them down before the land is swelled with injuries."

The testimony of the witnesses, mostly shoemakers, told the story of what had been going on in the shoe business in Hudson. The boss shoemakers had at first agreed to the prices set by the little union. Then, after the first big snowfall, when times began to be hard, the bosses told the men they would have to work for less. The shoemakers, true to their agreement, among themselves, walked out of the shops. Even Elisha Babcock—who had a big family to feed and keep warm—refused to go on working, though everybody knew how things were with him.

There were few disputes over the facts in the case. The whole town had seen these things happen. Josiah Sutherland and Henry Hogeboom kept reminding the nodding judges above them of how Chief

Justice Savage of the United States Supreme Court had settled a similar case—*People* v. *Fisher*—by upholding conviction. The eight shoemakers looked on in despair.

When young John Edmonds rose to speak, it seemed that the case was lost.

The twelve jurors—ten farmers, a merchant and a shoemaker—looked at the thirty-seven-year-old lawyer and wondered what he would say. They saw a tall, straight man whose eyes looked out at them with humor from under low, shaggy brows. They saw a big, straight nose, a firm mouth, a jutting chin. They saw a big head topped by a shaggy mat of wild, uncombed hair. And behind this man they saw the lean, smiling face and long body of Ambrose Jordan, already veteran of many a lost-cause fight for human rights.

John Edmonds began quietly and simply. He looked into the eyes of juror Elisha Lord and he said that every man, even a Chief Justice of the Supreme Court of the nation, could make a mistake. Justice Savage was a wise judge and a fine lawyer but he had made a mistake this time. Elisha Lord and the nine other farmer-jurors looked at each other. They understood this kind of talk. Even a smart farmer made errors in judgment sometimes. John Edmonds looked at juror-merchant Uriah Edwards and said that one of the greatest lawyers he knew of, Chancellor Kent, had said that probably the records of courts in this country are full of hasty and crude decisions that need correcting. Uriah Edwards understood that. He sometimes had to correct errors in his own bookkeeping. It was up to honest jurors to have the courage to make wrong acts right, said John Edmonds, and he looked at juror-shoemaker Robert Greene.

Then he began on a new tack. He said he had known these eight shoemakers a long time and they were honest, hardworking men. For years now, he said, they had tried day in and day out, to take care of their families while their wages were so low that all were poverty-stricken. When they got together to try to help each other by forming their society they found no law against it. Everyone who had known them realized, of course, that they were not criminals. All they wanted was a chance to work for enough wages to keep themselves and their families from want.

The prisoners looked at their anxious families sitting in the courtroom. Then they looked down at the floor with tears in their eyes. Josiah Sutherland was suddenly on his feet. He said that John Edmonds spoke of the Supreme Court of the United States in almost the same impudent spirit as the penny papers of New York City. Judge Savage had made the law his business all his life and he knew what he was talking about. It was the duty of the jury to find the defendants guilty if the evidence showed that the facts stated in the indictment were true.

Judge Wilcoxen then made a long charge to the jury. It was a smart speech and a smooth speech. It sounded mighty fair on the surface, but somehow everything he said seemed finally to come out against the shoemakers. He wound up by saying that if the shoemakers of Hudson had a right to combine to raise wages, then other workers all over the United States would have the same right. It was a question, he said, whether the control of labor in this manner throughout the country did not have a tendency to injure trade. Everybody had guessed where he stood by then.

The jurors filed out. Hopelessly the prisoners—Jonathan Cooper, Kenneth Defries, Frederick Brush, Robert Lawton, Herman Stoddard, John Marcellus, Sydney Wandle, and Elisha Babcock—awaited the outcome.

They did not wait long. Twenty minutes later their amazed ears heard the words—"Not guilty!"

They had "rescued the rights of the mechanics from the grasp of Tyranny and Oppression." Organized labor had won its first victory for the freedom of the working man.

5

Matthew Lyon

American history teaches us that time and again when government leaders have taken advantage of a widespread prejudice to deprive an unpopular citizen of his civil rights, they have been punished by loss of their own political power. The people of this country have at times been so carried away by the emotion of the moment that they have lent their support to some scheme or other meant to get around or to contradict the Bill of Rights. Once they have had a chance to think things over, however, they have admitted their errors and tried to make mincemeat of the men who led them astray.

Back in 1798 Alexander Hamilton, who was the smartest of all the Federalist Party leaders, told the Federalists they were making a mistake in passing the Alien and Sedition Laws, but President John Adams and the Federalist-dominated Congress were too angry to listen to him. The Democrat-Republicans had said too many stinging things about the government. Some of them, the Federalists thought, had been suggested by foreigners, particularly by "French philosophers" who had been wandering around the country preaching radical versions of Freedom, Equality, Fraternity. Others had come out of the pure cussedness of the Democrat-Republicans.

Whatever had been the source of the insults, the Federalists raged, they should not go unpunished. So they passed a law which said that the President could order all aliens that he judged dangerous to the peace and safety of the United States to leave the country. If an accused alien could not satisfy the President that he was harmless, he would have to leave the United States or be imprisoned for as long as three years. If but one man, the President, suspected aliens of being "dangerous" (whatever that might mean) they had to go back where they said they came from—or to jail.

The President's house.

As for the impertinent Democrat-Republicans the Federalists had a cure for them, too. They passed the Sedition Act which made it a crime punishable by imprisonment and fine for anyone to speak or publish "false, scandalous and malicious" sentiments tending to discredit the United States or its officers or to excite the hatred of the people against them. The idea seemed to be, moreover, that the Federalists, being in power, would determine what was "false, scandalous and malicious." They did not know at the time that the Federalist Party had committed suicide by passing these Acts. They found it out when election time came around. The passing of the Alien and Sedition Acts elected to the Presidency the man whom they regarded as America's most dangerous radical, Thomas Jefferson. It made the Federalist Party so unpopular that it did not survive Jefferson's administration.

Our history proves that the people of the United States believe too strongly in freedom of thought, freedom of speech, freedom of

the press ever to forsake them for the slaveries imposed by dictator-
ships. They will not be fooled when the crackpots begin shouting that
a man who criticizes the government is a traitor. They know that we
have got along pretty well so far with everybody considering it his
duty to say just what he thinks about the government. They know
that this is the democratic way and they are satisfied that it is a better
way than that of putting all power into the hands of a single despotic
leader. We should all remember the fate of the Federalist Party at
the end of the eighteenth century. They tried to win power by adopting such laws as a dictator might put into effect. They were destroyed.

This is the story of how it happened, the story of what we can
expect in America whenever a man's civil rights are taken away from
him by the majority in power. It is the story of Matthew Lyon of
Vermont.

Matthew was an Irishman, born in County Wicklow, "the vale in
whose bosom the bright waters meet." He was brought to Connecticut
when he was eight years old. There was a legend that he was appren-

The Capitol — Washington.

Capture of Fort Ticonderoga.

ticed to Tabez Bacon of Woodbury, but High Hannah of Litchfield wanted the boy and traded Tabez a pair of young bulls for him. By the time the boy was twenty-one, he had worked out his apprenticeship, and married a niece of that wild harum-scarum of the north, Ethan Allen. A few years later Matt Lyon was one of Uncle Ethan's Green Mountain Boys when they scrambled up and over the walls of Fort Ticonderoga.

After Gentleman Johnnie Burgoyne had surrendered at Saratoga, Matt felt the country was safe enough for him to leave the Army. He settled down in Vermont and began to make money. By 1783 he was the most distinguished citizen of Fair Haven and had an interest in the town's iron works, the paper factory, the printing press, the lumber company. About this time his wife died. A year later he married a widow named Beulah Galusha. It took him five years more to be elected to Congress on the Republican ticket, for New England was mostly Federalist.

When Matthew Lyon came to Philadelphia where Congress was in session, he was fighting-mad at President John Adams and the members of his "court" because of all their pretensions to royal splendor and aristocratic blood, and he said so. He made the Federalists so angry that they looked for a chance to get back at him by charging him with breaking the Sedition Law which they had passed to take care of just such cases.

They whooped with delight when they came upon one of Lyon's letters published in a Vermont newspaper. In it he had said that so far as the President was concerned, "when I shall see the efforts of that power bent on the promotion of the happiness and accommodation of the people, the Executive shall have my zealous and uniform support; but whenever I shall on the part of the Executive see every consideration of public welfare swallowed up in a continual grasp for power, in an unbounded thirst for ridiculous pomp, foolish adulation, and selfish avarice . . . I shall not be their humble advocate."

Hastily the Federalists added to this letter other similar evidences of Matthew Lyon's having violated the Sedition Law. A horseman raced fifteen miles through a cold October night to warn him that a jury made up mostly of Federalists was meeting in Rutland to indict him. His friends urged him to leave town, but he said calmly that he would not go. The next evening a deputy marshal came to Fair Haven and arrested him.

On the following morning Matthew Lyon presented himself in Rutland for trial. He had a hard time finding a lawyer who would defend him. When the trial got under way everybody there knew what the result would be. Federalist District Attorney March shouted that Matthew was guilty of a horrible crime, while in the jury box Federalist Jurors Bildad Orcutt, Jabez Ward, Ephraim Dudley, Joshua Goss, Elisha Brown, Moses Vail, and others listened with the light of vengeance gleaming in their eyes.

After the prisoner had spoken for two hours in his own defense, Federalist Judge Paterson told them that Matthew had made a speech "calculated to excite their pity" and clearly suggested to them that they bring in a verdict of "guilty of the high crime of opposing the Executive." After the formality of an hour's deliberation they did just that.

"Four months' imprisonment," said the judge, "and a fine of one thousand dollars."

At once Federalist Marshal Fitch took charge of his prisoner, ordered him about in an insulting manner, and arranged for his transfer to the jail at Vergennes, about forty-five miles away. Then, with the marshal triumphantly leading the way and two deputies, armed with pistols, following, Matthew Lyon rode as a common criminal to Vergennes—there to be jailed in a filthy 16 by 12 cell that had been used for punishing horse thieves, counterfeiters, and other felons. The Federalists had triumphed—or thought they had.

But something had suddenly gone wrong. Against this lonely prisoner were the President of the United States, his cabinet and advisers, the ruling political party—and yet in a twinkling he had more power than they. For the people of the United States had become aware that a man had been put in jail for saying what he thought about the government.

A whispering went around. It grew into a growl, then a roar. America is not made that way, the people shouted. Anybody can say what he thinks in this country. All at once the Federalists found themselves in the fix of the backwoodsman who got into a wrestling match with a bear and did not dare let go. All over the nation the people who had fought a war for their civil rights were demanding that these rights be recognized.

Down in the Carolina country John Taylor was passing around his big hat to raise the money to pay Matt Lyon's fine. In Virginia, Thomas Jefferson and General Stevens Thompson Mason were doing the same thing. In the hills and fields that surrounded the little jail at Vergennes, the Vermont farmers were working hard to find an extra shilling to give neighbor Apollos Austin toward Neighbor Lyon's release.

Neighbor Anthony Haswell, editor of the *Vermont Gazette,* was himself put in jail for helping along the good work by writing that

Sketch by Gregor Duncan

A petition for remission of Lyon's fine was presented to President Adams.

John Adams was a "hard-hearted savage" who had been "elevated to a station where he can satiate his barbarism on the misery of his victim." A petition for remission of Lyon's fine signed by thousands of Vermonters was presented to President John Adams.

"Has Matthew Lyon signed it?" asked John Adams.

"No, Mr. President."

"Penitence before pardon," said the President curtly.

A good many of the Green Mountain Boys could not sign their names to the petition (they had never been taught to write) but they thought of another way of getting their comrade out of prison—The Ticonderoga way. They showed up outside the Vergennes jail one day and said:

"Just say the word, Matt, and we'll tear this thing stone from stone."

But Matthew Lyon had too good sense to say the word. He said that loyal citizens obey the laws of their country whether they think them good or bad. If the laws are bad, they work toward getting them repealed—they do not break them.

So the Lyon of Vermont, as his sarcastic enemies had named him, stayed in jail while his persecutors saw their powers slipping away from them as the people of the country got their dander up. The frantic Federalists even tried a scheme to get Matthew to walk out of the jail unobserved, but he was too smart for them. One day his wife came to see him and it was suggested that he could leave with her and no one would be the wiser.

"He'll stay here if I have to stand sentinel over him myself," said Beulah Galusha Lyon.

Now the people of Vermont had the chance to defend Matthew Lyon with weapons even more powerful than the axes, crowbars, and muskets of the Green Mountain Boys. They could use their votes. The Federalists had plotted for the arrest and conviction of their enemy during a Congressional recess. They assumed that once they had Lyon locked in his cell he would be out of their way. No one, they whispered to one another, would vote for a "jailbird."

They could not have been more mistaken. Now the fighting Irishman in the dirty little cell was coming up for re-election to Congress.

Sketch by Gregor Duncan.

"I am the Scourge of Aristocracy," said Matthew Lyon, and the crowd cheered.

The eyes of all the nation were on Vermont. From the President down the Federalists rallied to the support of Williams, their candidate. The whole force and influence of the party in power were thrown into the Green Mountain state to defeat a time-serving convict.

And the "jailbird" licked them to a fare-you-well! Out of the farmhouses of Vermont, out of her village stores, out of her lumber camps, poured a stream of angry voters aching to tell the people of the United States that you could not make a Vermonter keep his mouth shut by throwing him in jail. When the votes had been counted, the prisoner of Vergennes had snowed his opponent under with a high drift of white ballots.

The four months of the sentence were almost up now. General Stevens Mason stuffed his saddlebags with more than a thousand dollars in gold and set out for Vergennes, claiming for Virginia the honor of paying Matthew Lyon's fine. It was too late, his friends told him—he could never get there in time. Yet, on the zero-cold morning of February 9, 1799, as Matthew Lyon stepped out of the Vergennes jail shouting "I'm on my way to Philadelphia!" Stevens Mason had already emptied his saddlebags and was leading the cheering.

Nearly every man in Vermont who believed in democracy and the rights of the people was there that day. The frozen surface of Otter Creek was smoother than the deep-drifted roads and the procession of crowded sleighs on it was more than ten miles long. When Matthew Lyon came out to freedom, cannons roared, horns blew, men shouted —and the great sound echoed through the snow-covered hills.

Now began a ride very different from the humiliating journey that had taken the convicted prisoner to jail. Out in front fluttered the Stars and Stripes. Riding behind the flag, Matthew Lyon acknowledged the cheers of a multitude. On they rode—through Tinmouth, where school children paraded in his honor and one spoke, hailing him as "our brave representative"; through Bennington, where good Republican Slade refreshed the party with cakes and hard cider while they sang songs and made speeches. Down through York State and Jersey they trotted, and the turnpikes were lined with cheering people who wanted a glimpse of the man who had gone to jail for exercising the rights of an American citizen.

"I am the Scourge of Aristocracy," said Matthew Lyon, and the people cheered and brought him gifts of big pies and bigger cheeses.

Philadelphia welcomed the "jailbird" Congressman with a shout. In a panic the Federalists tried to exclude him from his seat. They needed a two-thirds vote for that, more than sixty votes. The most they could muster was forty-nine. So Matthew Lyon rode from a Vermont jail into the Congress of the United States.

Months later Aaron Burr and Thomas Jefferson held an equal number of electoral votes for the Presidency and it fell to the House to resolve the tie. To Vermont came the opportunity of casting one of the deciding votes. The vengeance of the people was complete. Matthew Lyon cast a vote that made Thomas Jefferson, champion of civil rights, President of the United States. Even as he did so, the Federalist Party—party of monarchists and aristocrats and enemies of the freedoms granted by the Bill of Rights—fell dead as a doornail.

Whenever in these days an American politician begins shouting that the men who wrote the Constitution meant to give only "right-thinking" people like himself and those that agree with him freedom of expression, somebody ought to tell him this story.

William Lloyd Garrison, abolitionist.

6
William Lloyd Garrison

By the light of the first day of the year 1831 Bostonians read the title of a new journal—the *Liberator*. Under it William Lloyd Garrison had printed words that will not die while America lives—a battle cry of democracy: "I am in earnest—I will not equivocate; I will not excuse; I will not retreat a single inch; and I will be heard!" What Garrison said for his own cause ("the immediate enfranchisement of our slave population") American citizens are now proud to say for any cause they support.

It is an easy thing to persecute a fanatic. Even the people who agree with him in principle will not often come to his defense. "He does us more harm than good," they say smugly. "Let's go ahead carefully—let's keep our shirts on." Yet, the cause of human freedom has always owed more to the uncompromising than to the cautious. Joan of Arc was a fanatic. So was John Brown. So was William Lloyd Garrison.

Throughout the history of the United States no organized group of extremists was condemned with more bitterness than the Abolitionists. For more than thirty years before the War Between the States they spoke out for freeing the Negro slaves at once and for giving them the rights of all American citizens. In the 1830's and 1840's North and South alike cursed them for fools and rogues. Today they are the saints and martyrs of the cause we have come to call "The American Way."

Four years after the first copy of the *Liberator* had been published, New England's hatred of the Abolitionists (whom the journal represented) had grown to a frenzy. On October 21, 1835, the Boston Female Anti-Slavery Society had advertised that a meeting would be held at the offices of the *Liberator*. The anti-Abolition forces got the idea that the meeting was called to hear an English speaker against slavery, one George Thompson, and they sent out placards attacking "that infamous foreign scoundrel, Thompson," and stating "a purse of $100 had been raised by a number of patriotic citizens to reward the individual who shall first lay violent hands on Thompson, so he may be brought to the tar kettle before dark."

A mob gathered outside the *Liberator* offices that afternoon. George Thompson was not there, but the ladies of the anti-slavery society were. Though told they must leave at once to save themselves from danger, they bravely held their meeting before they walked out through groaning, hissing fellow citizens. "It was 5000 gentlemen against 30 Christian women," said Garrison. The city marshal, fearing a riot, spoke to the angry, milling crowd, telling them that George Thompson was not in town. In answer someone shouted that Garrison should take his place.

In an instant, the loud, menacing mob pushed forward. Some forced their way into the building and rushed to the locked office in which Garrison sat. They broke a panel in the door and stood and glared at him "like so many wolves." Finally they were driven from the building by the marshal and others. The crowd was so enraged by this that it became more dangerous than ever.

Now the Mayor of Boston played his part. Theodore Lyman was then forty-three years old, tall, handsome and distinguished. As he looked out over the crowd he recognized friends, for among the rioters were many of Boston's well-to-do citizens, members of the old town's best-known families. Garrison later described them as a "mob of gentlemen of property and standing."

The Mayor, a graduate of Phillips Exeter Academy and Harvard College, spoke with power. An eyewitness later remembered "his silvery voice and graceful elocution." While he begged the crowd to go to their homes and save the honor of Boston among cities, they shouted at him demanding the anti-slavery sign hanging from one of the windows of the *Liberator* offices. Theodore Lyman had a scheme in mind and he was playing for time. He ordered the sign given up. At once Henry Williams and John Dimmock tore it from its hangings and tossed it below.

While the crowd was tearing this prize to bits for souvenirs, the Mayor's scheme was working. Aided by friends, Garrison had quietly climbed out a back window and down a ladder into Wilson's Lane. Having reached the ground without being seen, he darted into a carpenter's shop. A high, wild cry came from one of the mob. He had seen the quick movement and guessed what it meant. There was a rush for the door.

Behind a pile of lumber on the second floor the manhunters found him.

"Throw him out the window," said one.

"No," said another, "let's not kill him outright."

They bound him with ropes and slid him down a ladder to the street. The ropes came off and the crowd grabbed him.

"I saw him," Thomas Nichols wrote, some years later, "his hat off, his bald head shining, his scanty locks flying, his face very pale, his clothes torn and dirty, and with a rope around his neck."

Now they dragged the helpless man toward Boston Common where they had planned to tar and feather him, then dye him with indelible

Anti-slavery meeting on Boston Common, 1851.

Culver Service

ink so that he would always look like the Negroes for whose rights he labored. Someone shouted that he should be hanged upon the great elm known as "The Tree of Liberty."

At that moment three men risked their lives to prevent so ironic a tragedy. They were not men who might have been picked out as likely to become heroes of a battle for civil rights. Two of them had little in common with the third, for their way of life could not have been more different from his. These were the brothers Dan and Buff Cooley, partners in a trucking business on India Street. The third was the aristocratic Mayor of Boston. None of them approved the opinions printed in the *Liberator*.

As the fierce hands of the mob tore at the lonely, frail person of William Lloyd Garrison, the two truckmen fought their way to him and for a moment beat off his assailants. With horny fists flailing about them they started leading Garrison toward City Hall.

"He shan't be hurt. He is an American!" shouted Buff Cooley.

"Don't hurt him. He is an American!" shouted brother Dan.

Then out of the maelstrom of angry people dashed the tall, powerful figure of Theodore Lyman.

"To my office!" he shouted to the Cooleys. With a rush the brothers responded, plunging through the crowd in front of the stumbling, beaten Garrison. The Mayor, fighting every step of the way, brought up the rear. Somehow, against overwhelming odds, they drove onward to the south door of the City Hall. It opened—and closed behind them. With a yell of rage the mob made for the north door. When they poured through it, the Cooleys and Garrison were already on the second floor and one man guarded the stairway—the Mayor. The silvery voice was strained now and the grace of elocution had given place to the grim sincerity of a man facing danger to his life.

"The law must be maintained," said Theodore Lyman staunchly, barring the mob from the stair. "I do not care for this man or cause —you know I do not sympathize with either—but the order of the city must be preserved if I must lay down my life on this spot."

Muttering, the mob retreated from the building. Upstairs friendly hands replaced Garrison's torn clothing with borrowed garments while the shouts outside grew louder and more ominous. The Mayor ordered a carriage brought up to the south door and guards sent down as if to protect Garrison's exit there. The crowd gathered about them. Then swiftly, with the Mayor in front, the Sheriff on one side and stout Ebenezer Bailey—armed with a strong umbrella—on the other, Garrison ran into a carriage waiting outside the north door.

"The coachman lashed his horses into the crowd," wrote Thomas Nichols, who was there. "They grasped the wheels to turn the carriage over; but as they seized both sides at once they only lifted it from the ground. They took out knives to cut the traces. The driver knocked them down with the loaded handle of his whip. The spirited horses dashed forward, the mob opened, and then ran yelling after the carriage. It was too fast for them. Up Court Street, down Leverett Street. Ponderous gates swung open—the carriage dashed in. The gates closed with a bang and Garrison was safe in Leverett Street Jail."

So ends the story of how a few men who believed in American principles saved a man, with whose ideas they disagreed, from a howling mob.

Culver Service

The mob dragged Garrison toward Boston Common.

Elijah P. Lovejoy

7

Elijah Lovejoy

On a sharp November evening two years after Mayor Lyman had rescued Garrison, a citizens' meeting was in progress in the Mississippi River town of Alton, Illinois. Solemnly the chairman of a committee read a report to his fellow citizens. "Without desiring to restrain the liberty of the press in general," he intoned, "it is indispensable that Mr. Lovejoy should not be allowed to conduct a paper and that he should retire from the charge of the Alton *Observer*."

Then, editor Elijah Lovejoy stood up to answer. He was a stocky man, broad and of medium height. His big brown eyes seemed to fill with light as he talked. Sometimes they gleamed with humor. Sometimes they burned with the zeal of the true crusader.

Since he had come from St. Louis to Alton in search of a more broad-minded public, Lovejoy had lost three printing presses at the hands of anti-Abolitionist mobs. Now he awaited a fourth and while he did so his fellow townsmen had prepared this silly statement which dared in the same sentence to refer to the Bill of Rights and to recommend the suppression of his newspaper.

Elijah Lovejoy spoke calmly and seriously at first. He said that he got no pleasure from opposing the majority of the townspeople on the question of slavery and that he had not, as his enemies charged, "held in contempt the feelings and sentiments of this community in reference to the question which is now agitating it." He asked only that his neighbors respect his rights as a citizen saying that his own actions were guided by higher motives "than either the favor or the fear of man."

Suddenly the dark eyes flashed and the words that had been quiet and slow poured from the editor's lips in a fiery flow.

"What, sir, I ask, has been my offense? Put your finger on it—define it—and I stand ready to answer for it. . . . Why am I threatened with the tar barrel? Why am I waylaid every day and from night to night, and my life in jeopardy every hour?" His strong voice trembled. Tears ran down his cheeks as he continued, "But what then? If the civil authorities refuse to protect me, I must look to God. And if I die, I have determined to make my grave in Alton."

The town was in a fever of waiting during the next few days. Every steamboat that blew for the Alton landing brought a crowd racing to the docks to see if the new printing press had arrived, if the anti-Abolitionists would destroy it.

On the cold clear night of Monday, November 6, 1837, a band of between forty and fifty believers in the freedom of the American press waited, armed with rifles and muskets, in Gilman's riverside warehouse. From downriver sounded the deep voice of the fancy white steamboat, *Missouri-Fulton*. As the big boat sidled into the docks the volunteer guards, many of whom were not Abolitionists, moved to the water's edge and watched the Negro deck hands bring the heavy machine ashore. At a safe distance a few rowdies hurled stones at them but there was no real disturbance as the press was hurried into the warehouse. Then the night was quiet.

So was the next day. The hours moved slowly. A cloud of dread hung over the dusty streets. As darkness again settled slowly over the river and town, the volunteer guards drifted toward the warehouse. The lamps had been burning in the windows of Alton for about two hours when most members of the party agreed that the present danger was over and went home. By ten o'clock only twelve men sat in the big building, a guard to wait the night out.

Suddenly there was a shot in the darkness outside, a rattle of stones against the wooden walls. Then loud voices were calling for Gilman, owner of the warehouse. Mr. Gilman went to a window above the river.

"We want that press!" shouted one of the mob.

"The mayor has told us we may rightfully defend it with our lives," said Gilman. "We shall do so."

Stones crashed through the windows. The crowd outside were

getting bolder. The little band of defenders could hear the clanging of the bell in the steeple of the Presbyterian church. There the slender and delicate body of the pastor's wife swung on the ropes as she tried to waken the people of Alton to their duty. No help came.

Outside there was the rattling crash of a volley and bullets zinged through the windows and smacked against the walls. Cautiously the twelve moved up to the shattered panes, raised their guns and fired. There was a cry, then long silence. The mob had run away leaving a dead man behind them.

They came back when they saw crowds from town streaming down the moonlit river bank toward them. They raised a ladder against the house, looked for a volunteer to climb it and set fire to the roof. With the usual cowardice of grown men in mobs, they chose fifteen-year-old "Okey" for the job. Flaring torch in hand, the boy went up the ladder and climbed the slant of the roof. He knelt a moment at the summit while the shingles leaped to flame beneath him.

The men in the warehouse smelled smoke and guessed what had happened. They opened the west door and looked out. All was quiet. On the north side of the building the mob shouted and danced. Five of the besieged suddenly rushed around the southwest corner of the house and fired at Okey. A bullet wiped out an eyebrow and Okey slid down the ladder in a hurry. The flames on the roof flickered out.

Then, as the five reloaded their guns in the doorway from which they had made their attack, Elijah Lovejoy joined them. The moonlight was around him as he stood there just inside the threshold. A man rose from behind a lumber pile a few yards away. He raised a double-barreled shotgun to his shoulder, took careful aim, and fired.

Lovejoy fell back, turned and crawled up the near-by stair to the counting room. There he died.

The guard inside the warehouse gave up the struggle after that. The mob promised them safe passage to their homes and then fired on them as they came out, but without hitting anyone. The corpse of Lovejoy lay on a cot near the rioters as they streamed into the building, grabbed the parts of the printing press and threw them into the Mississippi.

The members of the mob were happy the next day. They had

The Alton riot — from an old print.

showed the Abolitionists that they could not print their dangerous ideas in Alton. But after a week or so they were puzzled and hurt. Anti-Abolitionist and Abolitionist alike—all over the country—were denouncing them as murderers. Press and pulpit and common man all agreed with the Boston preacher William Ellery Channing who wrote: "An event has occurred which ought to thrill the hearts of this people as the heart of one man. A martyr has fallen among us to the freedom of the press. A citizen has been murdered in defense of the right of free discussion. . . . He has been murdered in exercising what I hold to be the dearest right of a citizen."

Lovejoy won. Today a nation calls him hero and martyr and cherishes his memory, a nation that is willing to risk its own life in defense of the principle which is described in his own words—words carved on his tombstone at Alton, Illinois: "But, gentlemen, as long as I am an American citizen, as long as American blood runs in these veins, I shall hold myself at liberty to speak, to write, to publish whatever I please on any subject—being amenable to the laws of my country for the same."

8

John Peter Altgeld

On the afternoon of May 4, 1886 about three thousand people of Chicago were gathered about a wagon in Cranes' Alley near Haymarket Square. Strikes in the plants of McCormick Reaper, the Pullman Palace Car Corporation, and the Brunswick-Bensinger billiard firm had been going on for some time in an effort to force the employers to grant their workers an eight-hour day. Sam Fielder was speaking from the wagon—speaking doggedly, for the crowd was smaller than he had expected and he feared a loss of interest in the cause. His hearers grew restless as he neared the end of his talk.

A block away a detachment of police waited. The big demonstration which they had been told to keep in order had not materialized. The faces of the bored officers brightened as they saw Mayor Harrison approaching. He spoke a few words to their commander, Inspector Bonbright. Those near enough to overhear smiled broadly. The Mayor had told the inspector to send his men home. The day's work was done.

The Mayor went on, turned a corner and was out of sight. Suddenly Bonbright gave the sharp order to fall in. The surprised men muttered their disappointment as they marched in military formation down the street toward the strikers.

Sam Fielder was bringing his remarks to a dull and discouraged close when he heard an interrupting voice. It was that of Police Captain William Ward at the head of the column. "I command you in the name of the people of the State of Illinois to immediately and peacefully disperse."

Witnesses disagreed about what happened after that. Some claimed Sam Fielder spoke defiantly, others that he merely said, "But we are peaceable." Whatever he might have said further was drowned out by a wild cry from someone in the crowd. A dark object hung in the air for a moment. There was a shattering explosion.

Some time later, when the crowd had dispersed under the fire of the police, Inspector Bonbright was able to check up on the casualties his unreasonable decision had led to. One officer was already dead. Seven had been fatally wounded. Sixty-seven had been injured.

A wave of fear swept the State of Illinois. No one knew who threw the bomb but somebody was going to have to suffer for it. The feeling was that these labor radicals were dangerous anarchists, capable of an armed uprising, and they should be taught a lesson. Thus, by the end of the month thirty-one believers in the eight-hour day had been indicted for the murders committed by the bomb thrower. Two weeks later eight of the thirty-one went on trial for their lives. No one seemed to know why or how these eight were chosen. A month went by and no evidence of the identity of the criminal had been presented. Nevertheless, the prisoners at the bar were declared guilty and seven were sentenced to be hanged.

Before the day set for the executions one of the seven cheated the gallows by hanging himself in his cell and the sentences of Sam Fielder and Michael Schwab were commuted to life imprisonment. Then, on November 11, four men were hanged in the United States of America for a crime of which they had not been proved guilty. All over the nation frightened people approved this violation of one of the rights guarded as most sacred by the Constitution—the right to a fair trial. Few believed poor August Spies who said while he waited for the noose to be put about his neck: "There will come a time when our silence will be more powerful than the voices you strangle today."

The frightened people of Illinois had thought that by executing somebody (guilty or not) for the terrible crime they would achieve peace of mind. They soon found they were mistaken. The killing of four innocent men did not sit well on their consciences. The knowledge of their error made them more frightened than ever. All over the state men ranted and raved against the "anarchists" in the effort to make themselves believe that they had done well in punishing men not for their crimes but for their ideas.

Years went by and four of the indicted thirty-one remained in prison—living monuments to one of America's greatest crimes against her own national principles. Intelligent and honest men rallied about them and strove to secure their pardon, but the people of the state of Illinois were still too shocked by the tragedy to listen to reason. They denounced the champions of justice. They said that whether the prisoners were guilty or not they had got what was coming to them. Then a new governor—a bearded quiet man, John Peter Altgeld, was elected Governor of Illinois. Few had known where he stood on the question of pardoning the prisoners. He had never, as a private citizen, lent his name to their cause. But, while he was working toward the governorship John Peter Altgeld had been doing a lot of thinking.

After his election in 1892 the men who were fighting to see justice done renewed their efforts. The campaign had become a world issue by now. Over in London an excited young man was walking the streets demanding peremptorily from passers-by that they sign a petition for pardons for the faraway prisoners. He showed them his own name, signed with a flourish at the head of the list—George Bernard Shaw. The versatile English artist and craftsman, William Morris, was writing to his colleague, Robert Browning, begging the support of the best-known poet of his time for aid to the persecuted Americans. And a young lawyer named Darrow climbed the steps of the capitol at Springfield to see the Governor of his state.

"Go tell your friends," said John Peter Altgeld, "that when I am ready I will act but I will do what I think is right."

Earnestly the Governor sought to find support for the cause of justice among the big corporations which were influential in the state. They refused to be interested. Knowing the liberal tendencies of the distinguished lawyer Lyman Trumbull, Altgeld sent his best friend, George A. Schilling, to ask Trumbull to petition him for the long overdue pardon.

"The time will come," said Trumbull to Schilling, "when mankind will look back upon the execution of the anarchists as we of this day look back upon the burning of the witches in England," but he refused to make the petition.

Then George Schilling went back to his friend and said:

"Governor, unless you are willing to do this all alone—without regard to consequences, and thereby serve notice that there is at least one man in public life that the corporations have not cowed—the situation is hopeless. Then we might as well drop it!"

John Peter Altgeld walked up and down the room for a while after that. Then he stopped and looked for a long time at the picture hanging above his desk—the picture of another bearded man, a fellow townsman once—Abraham Lincoln. Deliberately, at length, he sat down.

Altgeld looked for a long time at the picture.

"Schilling," he said, "we don't need them! We don't need them!"

Young Brand Whitlock was the secretary to the Governor on the June morning he ordered the pardons made out. In his reminiscences he tells how calm Altgeld was when he signed the papers—how the Chicago banker, Dreier, burst into tears of joy when they were given to him to take to the prison at Joliet. He says the Governor knew full well the storm of protest that would come but he was not troubled.

The storm broke. All the frightened people of the nation railed at the Governor of Illinois. "Governor Altgeld has encouraged anarchy, rapine and the overthrow of civilization," screamed the *Toledo Blade*. "The document read almost as if the Governor himself were an anarchist," said the *Nation*. At Harvard's annual alumni dinner in Cambridge, Robert Todd Lincoln, son of Abraham, disgraced his father by mouthing: "It is for you Harvard men to stand firm in the midst of such dangers to the republic." The Governor of Illinois was insulted by many of his friends, ignored by others. Throughout all the furor he moved quietly and with dignity, the ghost of a smile tugging at his firm lips. The pardon document had expressed his ideas on the trial. He would not explain further. It said that the trial jury was packed for the purpose of convicting the defendants, that the jurors had out of their own mouths admitted their incompetence, that the defendants were not proved guilty, that the judge was prejudiced.

Only once did John Peter Altgeld speak out from his heart about his decision. It was when he stood at the grave of his mother and he was talking to the folks he had grown up with in Little Washington Community among the Ohio hills. His words had the simplicity of greatness, his manner the sincerity of a true believer in American ideals:

"Those fellows did not have a fair trial and I did what I thought was right."

This is a good time to remember those simple words of his. It is a good time to remember other words, written by another great man of Springfield about him. Vachel Lindsay, when he was a little boy, saw John Peter Altgeld enter the state capitol as Governor. When he was a man Lindsay expressed the ideas of hundreds of thousands of Americans when he wrote his tribute to the man who cheerfully gave up his political future to be able to say: "I did what I thought was right." Now Lindsay too is dead, but America chants his words for John Peter Altgeld:

"Sleep softly . . . eagle forgotten . . . under the stone.
Time has its way with you there, and the clay has its own.

'We have buried him now,' thought your foes, and in secret rejoiced.
They made a brave show of their mourning, their hatred unvoiced.
They had snarled at you, barked at you, foamed at you day after day.
Now you were ended. They praised you . . . and laid you away.

The others, that mourned you in silence and terror and truth,
The widow bereft of her crust, and the boy without youth,
The mocked and the scorned and the wounded, the lame and the poor,
That should have remembered forever, . . . Remember no more.

Where are those lovers of yours, on what name do they call,
The lost, that in armies wept over your funeral pall?
They call on the names of a hundred high-valiant ones,
A hundred white eagles have risen, the sons of your sons.
The zeal in their wings is a zeal that your dreaming began.
The valor that wore out your soul in the service of man.

Sleep softly . . . eagle forgotten . . . under the stone.
Time has its way with you there, and the clay has its own.
Sleep on, O brave-hearted, O wise man that kindled the flame—
To live in mankind is far more than to live in a name,
To live in mankind, far, far more . . . than to live in a name." *

* "The Eagle that is Forgotten" (John P. Altgeld, born December 30, 1847; died March 12, 1902), from Vachel Lindsay, *Collected Poems*. By permission of the Macmillan Company, publishers.